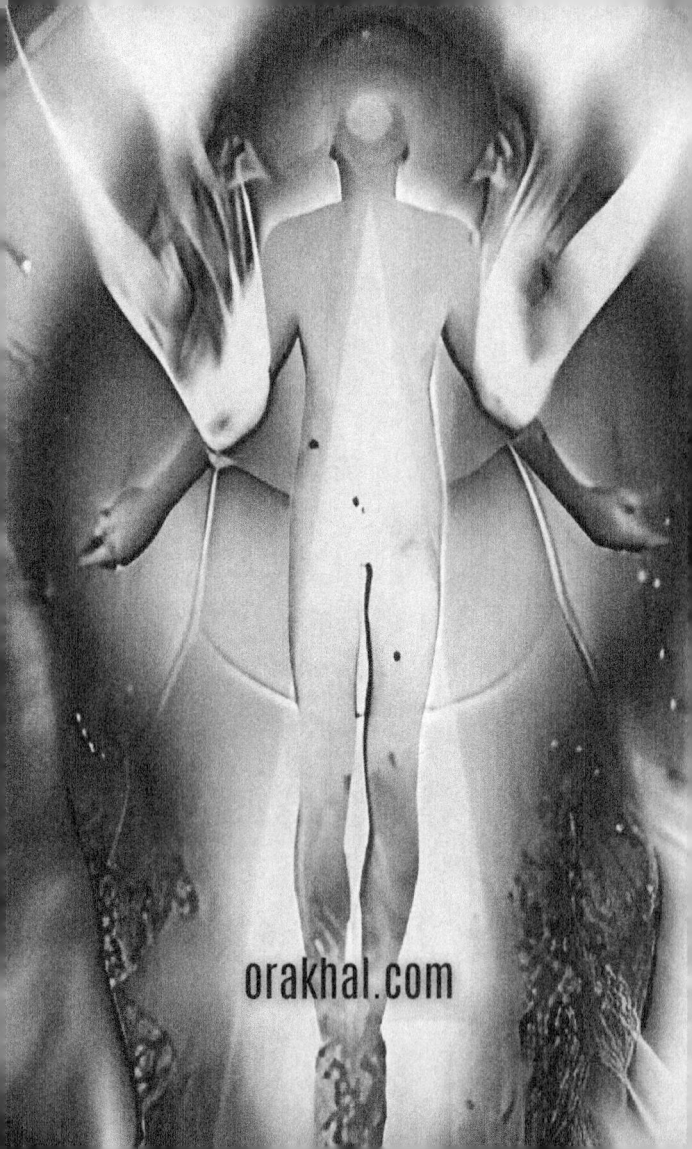

defeats the feel

you can not feel
what you are wanting to feel
by way of not feeling it

fooling your self

habits thrive
on self justification

conjuring thoughts that allow
you self afflict with good reason

and your light nature
has no mercy on a body preying upon itself
with its own mind and conscience

is clear all the way through
once you stop contradicting
your own energy of your own being
spinning it to play with

mind games

everything playing to your mind
as your imagination
is energy of your body

to be allowed
and integrated

not what
thought thinks

could have you
believe its not

so you abuse
yourself with it

mental combat

do you not own the thought
and feel its energy as your light

then you have no power
to shift its influence over you

infinite waters

space is full
of worlds and being

same as an
ocean is full of drops

shown you once you understand
the ocean animating the drops

stepping into your light nature

light naturally exhumes you
once you stop playing
with your thought shadows

you do not get to your light nature
through your thought shadows
playing you

meaning nothing

is more
than it means

had you met death

you would not
live it as light

and prepare
for its bounty

space ships

are made
of space

making a mess of it

chaos trying to
order disorder

causes
chaos

is not the same
as ringing order
out of chaos

as you step
in you are in it

as you
step out

you are in it

as you are light
you play it

as you
are space

you are played

the rub

you think things rub off on you
same way you think your skin
keeps you together or you might
spill out all over the place

space is charged
through not of your body

your light nature is not being felt by you
but through the human body resisting it
once it lets up

is spatially exhumed
as a no body of light

your future
is easy to predict

are you
living it now

mind

is a reaction
to your light nature
animating it

matters
not what dies

matters only
what lives to

space
untouched

is your god

not the
goings on of it

self suicide without knowing

all the dark drama
playing out of your reality

is the fuel you
use to kill yourself with

thinking it is
not your problem

ask self

does your mind and feeling shift
because you know something

or not know it

a weight
that lifts you up
as you carry it along

feels strange
but true

over a weight
that weighs you down
trying to drop it

back up

know more by way of
knowing less not more

your mind has the look

your
light

the
sight

think you get it and you dont

space
lives all

full of
emptiness

not fullness

wisdom
has no source

and only death
keeps it alive

superior being

is less
by way of light

and more
by way of space

what humans suffer or not
as light being

is based on spatial principles
not light principles

clarity

not quality

the evil nature

suffering occurs
at the hands of evil thought

not evil humans

or you are
done for

convincing your self you die

you shall not
suffer more than death
as a human

are you keeping it
clear and in order as you go
of your light nature

shall suffer you
more than death
are you not

if you want remedy

stop seeking
it through relief

why

because that
is the effect playing you

not the cause

and to charge
clear a remedy

means to stop
playing with the effect

as the cause

the no where clause

for dark light things to be
truly deactivated and clear

in regards to physical
reality and law

it can not exist in the
back of your mind

is where it is all
playing from

missing out

have you not ever
thought to think that your good nature
could could be creating what is not

seems an abnormal
way to be thinking

as nothing dark
ever is your own
thought and light

as most
humans see it

is a play
must be unearthed
are you to survive your self

the sly light

the most
dangerous humans
are not the obvious ones
doing it for the wrong reason

are the ones doing it
for the right reason

taking a power
to gain one back

redeeming your nature

you may of lost
a lot of blood

but you have not ever
lost a drop of light

is not possible
on the whole

as space
takes up your charge

an immutable truth

leaves you
nothing to go on

the emotional bot

human gets emotional
about its own thought

suffice to say it is
easy to program and motivate it
to be emotional about a binary life
has none

based on its
own principles at play

hanging out to dry

are you feeling
others thoughts

then you are not
feeling your own

the fact you think you feel
others thoughts as your own
is your issue requires a clean up

vanish the mental
suggestion that you have no control over
your own thoughts thinking you
and make amends with your own mind

as the cock crows

how ever
dark life gets

it is always
made of light

and space
charging it

rules
the roost

how to be
nice to the shadow

take comfort
in knowing it is your own light play
creates one of your self

tell the story you have always told

and you are lived the life
you have always lived

not playing with
your thought about others

takes you
out of the game

and not
their game

as you press
and play your own
thought energy at others

draws their thought
out of them at you

a twisted affection

it is not normal to worry sick
about your self as others
and blame them for it
assuming its love

a free one

space nurtures
your clarity

not your thoughts
and feelings

nurture
your self

being your thought is easy

being your mind
aware of the thought

trickier

being your light
animating your mind
aware of the thought

even more so

being space
charging your light
animating your mind
aware of the thought
yet clear of its influence

the end game

a tongues bite

how foolish the human mind
is to believe it has good reason
to question others with its own answer

the hearing mind

no mind is speaking to
what it is talking about

is only talking
at what it speaks

feeling others thoughts

despite what
you think

it is
all yours

or you are holding
your thought apart

and being
played by it

the simplicity of wisdom

wisdom is simple
not complicated by
simple minds

the architect
of all mind is light
ordered of space

not light animation
ordered of thought

be the best you
by way of dropping
what does not apply to that

not by way of the lesser you
trying to be your best

the effect of thought

your thought is not being cast
at the things and people you see

apart

your light is animating
your thought are the things
and people you see as you

mind readers

know people
as your own mind and thought

before seeing and
hearing them out

the is how a true light being
learns to communicate

not by way of pressing
thought energy at one another

leaders of a free world

are not going
to wear human faces

is a higher purpose
to win over something

then it is a
lower purpose

the good

you think
something is good

because it
suits you to

not because
its good

the kind of
good you want

is one you take no credit for
nor give any a way to

as all
is spoken for

answers and responses

a question is always
put to your self

not the one
you ask it of

has no business
knowing what is right
or not for you

playing your part

the human breed
wanting to rule over and oppress people
are nominated appointed
and played into that position
by the human not living
its own light movie

installing players in it
coincides with this failure to
take up its own light and live it

rather plays it from the side lines
off what others have active of the field

catch it playing you first

and you will not
play with it so much

the human mind tends
to react to the thought
before looking at it and
tasting it as its body energy

a mental state and space
you have to deliberately practice
and cultivate incessantly

to integrate any energy
you play against you

real joy is not having
to feel what you are not
because you do not

get this

everything is alive
because of what its not

not because
of what it is

the flick of an eye

exercise watching things and people
without talking in your head
about that and them

and make it a golden rule
until what you say in the head
is spoken clear

and not speaking
without your consent

plain to see

giving out at something
you went looking for
and divided your self on

is hardly
a wise play

does something or someone you
happen on tick you off

then stop
playing with it as you

do not blame
at it for playing you

taking you to task

as you get
that you animate all things
of your own light nature

through your
human nature

you will no longer play around
with the notion things are not you

your eyes distract you
because you see of light
and translate it into all sorts of distorted things
through the thought it is something its not

hold firm to the physical
nature and reality as your life

not your light
animating it

anger is fear

as it signifies
something you can not control

controlling you

is a
weak spot

not a
strength

hear me out

the world can not hear you
talking to your self

however loud you yell
it shall always be into
your own ear canal you go

until you are spoken silent
and the word pours forth without an echo

the win over

try and detect
are you judging things
people do and say

to do and
say it better

a tricky little
shadow tactic

or being complementary
because you feel lesser
has the same throw

the sum total

madness
thinks its mad

and
did it not

and just
be mad

it would be
better served its sanity

he did not know he died

as he had not yet been lived
and come to know death

how to be something
yet not a part to it

being clear allows what is
and is playing out
untouched to you

choosing
sides does not

home alone

you can not read
some body as them

ever

you think
you can

because you believe
as your own thought
that they live your
mind and body

not you

chasing your fire

it is not possible to play with
energy you can not see
yet put a face to

and not be it

sets many a light off
of your own fire

quantum entanglement

quantum
energy is space

not its
light essence
at play

a world feeling sorry for you
means only it is feeling sorry for itself

not you

do not be tricked into
believing you resolve your own energy
through the world reflects it back at you

is not your
own light movie

but will be

are you one revealing
all your secrets
and playing
it that way

picture
this effect

the human mind
stops asking questions
and allows space be the answer

not having to
show up with one

a lame excuse

knowing
people are wrong

is easy
to be right about

needing to feel it

i must work out
why i feel what i feel

think what i think

is the number one reason
a body side steps space and
locks itself into its own play

and also how atmospheric
light shadows and energy
manipulate and play you

the birth of human

space
charges light

animates
dna

expresses
the physical being

made of light
charged by space

what is life without the chance of justice

life

simply

spatial order is
not justified through order
and disorder

this is the trouble
with humans and dark light

learn to leave the untouchable
alone and it will serve you clear a life cycle

be at it apart and you shall
suffer your own light nature

down on your light

you defy what you animate
as your own thought defied

nothing more stirs your fire
but your own interpretation
of your own thought

held for or against you
as something or somebody else

dark matter
may not be observed

because
it is the observer

same way
you can not see your mind
having and being a thought

nor the eye
you look through

space has no eye
and is the dark matter and charge
births all light and life through one

the knowing mind

when you
really know

you do
not need to

and until
that occurs to one

you are just knowing
for knowings sake

the end of an eye

what the human
is searching for

is its own light animating
what it is searching for

looping on
its own creative effects
calling it self discovery

is exactly what took it out
the last time it was rebooted

have you no light on

blood is all
you get to drink

feeler

had you no thought
of what a thing is

what
would it be

eye o eye

everything
you look at

is in
your eye

not being
looked at

wisdom as light

shapes every
word spoken

through
tongues of fire

stolen of
worlds unbroken

it is a rare one

masters saying everything
with nothing to say

causal light

the human body

being animated
by what is inside it

not outside

explains more as to why it displays
and plays the dark game it plays into the world

not yet aware
and knowing
it is played

inner cycles

you affect
everything and everyone
you ever touched

as you come
clear a light

as its of the spatial field
tells every story ever spun and lived

now time
yet timeless cycles

shift to match the play
of past present and future

on every side of the fence

just because
you get it

does not
mean you are it

as many humans
use what you get to
win over each other

not combine light

changes everything

you
playing
them

as
you

who is playing who

you
play you

and the
players you play
you play as you

thinking they are
players not you

is the reason you
are played so easily by
and through one another

death becomes your teacher

dying is the key

not playing with
the untouchable force
lives clear through you

a light

is
space

the not being of being

it is not just that you know things
in your mind and see that as your own reality

you put that there
to know and see

animate your life
through your own thought

something an observers mind can not fathom
looking at the thought it thinks it is not being

no eyes no see

light
blindness
is not caused
by what you see

blindness is chosen
through what you can not see

no two sides to a story

as you are
the only one writing it

a human player
in its movie
knows this

ones not

play all the characters
yet assume it is not any of them

leaving you behind

are you
reaching for nothing

you are being lived and brought
to where you try to get to

about turns

what is physical
catches up and on
with what is not

not the other
way around

you have no face
but space to go by

truth has an edge

cuts most humans
lying to the self

how she feels his eyes

the inner most nuances
tickle a bodys heat

comes of the
body it tickles

despite the
interference latches
on to play

come off it

life is clear with
nothing you did not do

as much as it is
with everything you did

basic instinct

dreams are what
waking people bring to life

and sleeping people
wake up from

using not abusing you

the more angry you get at what you feed on
the more opportunity you have
to integrate your shadow
and be done with it

that is

are you admitting your the one
playing with the shadow of your light

not the information
and thought built into it

a negative reaction
means you fear your light

accusing thoughts betray
the mind and body
of the thinker

and the thinker
thinks its the thought

why it hurts to be wrong

because your light is always spot on
about what you think you know
that you don t

odd balls

no human has to expel
from its reality
what animates it

it does this
because it has no idea
it is animating its reality
and all the players in it

are either friend or foe
as far as it can tell

not ever
its self

how you look beautiful

**is how
you feel unseen**

space requires no reason
to love and forgive you

a light being accepts the charge
and order of space
acquits it by law

or not

lands it on the cycle
best suited to its advancement
as a light being

the human being a
secondary or animated nature

shadow walkers

let humans
attempting to play you

walk their energy
through you clearly

not all over you

so they fall
over their own wobble

not yours

take it or leave it

but dare not believe
you are given it

it really is futile
to be right about anything

requires one to take
a left approach

the play of players

do you reject the notion
you animate your own light movie

you will not understand the dynamic
between you and the players in it
you play

will use them rather
to mess you all up

no way not to

space as light
will produce you any chaos
you wish to order

by way of
trying to order it

mental games

your mind can not change
a thought it does not want

without having
one it does not want

spatial milking

thought
essence is light

not imagination

and to witness all thought play
not be it as the image in your head
and emotion in your body

allows space absorb the energy
and free you of any thought
burning back on your light
causing the effect

what god is

space will tear you asunder
are you unable to embody it

and not as a
horrible father and judge

as a
renewer of light

orders exactly what is best for all
through the alls own chaotic effects

what changes you

is that you
try to change

plague your body
with a desire to satisfy it

and it will turn on you
for no longer being able to feed it

more to you
than meets the eye

should it turn
out to be the case

that you are
the alien inside you

what then

upside of down

anything
that dies

lives

apart from the human
thinks it is living

experiences death
through a body resisting

not living

does energy
require a body to live

or does a body
need energy to live

energy is all

great confusion and chaos
comes through the ordering of energy
through form

is energy
not form

no god exists

but for light
assigning space the role

not space
assigning light

the all is all

the drops in an ocean
however lit up and powerful

are not ever going to wield power
over the oceans charge

now you know
nothing is everything

what you
gonna do with nothing

a no brainer

no body wants your reality
to be the reason they live

is a mathematical
impossibility

as they animate
your reality as their own

space does not touch you

lives you un touched
as you touch
your self

you know

what
you do
not think

hey shadow leave
your light alone

imagine that

a light trying
to win over its own shadow
trying to win over its own light

nothing blows your mind

but the
fresh empty air

playing it safe

the human playing
its reality out through others realties

not sticking to
its own light movie

is what has and will destroy
many do you not cop on to this

safety in numbers

is the one
not powerful enough

then the many
shall spoil

why you can not choose

a choice
is chosen you

of what
is not choosing

intelligent life

is nothing
it knows it is

what comes
of nothing

is all

renders
a lesser thing more

having to defend knowledge

shows one
knows little about it

watchers

do not be so
quick to be your self

where all your
glitches and problems are kicking off

rather try watching
and observing your human self

of your light nature
not pitching things at and through it

be the space watching you
not one feeling having and living you

hounds out of bounds

a mature human light being
will not pester other players
in its own light movie

as it realises the consequences
are its own creative effects

reality on play back
deserves it exactly what
it plays with apart

what makes your blood boil

is the
temperature
of your own light

not the
spatial press

one up on others

do not be a fool
trying to win over
your own intelligence
through others coming
into your mind and life

is a difficult
thing not to do

but a very silly play
threatens your own security blanket
and holds you back from your own path

the stand alone self

is natural to battle
your self in your mind as others
as you are coming clear and waking up

because you have since birth
been playing the part of others as your self

and now you are beginning to
withdraw from that and play you just
of your own light nature

and be totally
aware of it

every thought your mind throws up

is made
of light

not
thought

and as you
perceive it as such
you will not be inclined to
play and hurt yourself with it

what keeps the shadows off you

are the spatial giants of charge
and light over your shoulder
cradling your fire

what keeps the light
off you

are the spatial giants of charge
and shadow over your shoulder
cradling your light

life threats

spatially clear
and charged up light beings
do not make threats

carry out
spatial orders
of law

of what charges
through their light being
spills into the light arena
charged lesser and darker a light

overlooked

what you live
lives you

as much
as you live it

in fact

more so for humans
much of the time

thinking its life
is apart from its self

what you get is
what you give yourself

period

nothing is
apart from you
creating what you
animate and play with
apart from you

click of thick

human as its self
animates through its fellow humans
the realities its fellow humans
use to destroy it with

the fire of change

a fire is merciless
and rips through all things

unless you
become the fire

a true experience of space

is not ever
applied to it

death always dies

sounds obvious

until you
realise you create
it of your own light

is not

applauding your self for knowing

impressed by your own
likes and dis likes

run through the mental
words and worlds of thought
as other players dictate your energy

is not a very clear
light playing its self
now is it

thought sees
its way through you

are you able
to live not think it

giving people what
you think you want

think of it
this way

you play your own light movie
and you play the players in it with you

why then would you ever think
they will and must play you
any different to what you
are playing them

the magic breath

best not be looking inside you
for what is out side you

or you end
up outside you
looking in

and you do not want to be
watching the movie you are in

you want to be animating it
of your light of space

the only way
to stop being played

is to not play
with what plays you

why does evil exist

the same
reason space exists

only what
light lives

not accepting
it as space

creates the
anti life of space

pays to know

life is happy
with you not happy

in fact it prefers it
so it can happily live you

around and around we go

being alive to
the spatial masters
as a human light principle

means you can
not die even if you do
and are cradled by their expectations
tuned into yours

all gods must die

for not being
the one lives all gods

it is not
arrogant to be wiser

it is arrogant
to believe others are not
wise enough to know better

puts and plays them
into that position
as your self

only ever as smart
as you think others are

how to die
to your self in 4 words

be lived
by space untouched

how to resist effectively

understand

no player
in your light movie
is out of wack

as you animate
and play them

and you shant
need to resist your self
as any body or anything

how easy it is

to live
something you know

yet do not
think you live

a problem with you

is some body
elses problem

until it is not
a problem with you

foundational laws

you are
your thought reality

and or

you are your
light reality

both charged by space not thinking
ringing forth the physical effects you live

you live your thought

not the reality coming of
what you think you live

the being

did you not know your thought
as your body feeling it
nor believe what it says

and sustain this position
as a primary mindset

your light
would become you

and no thought could
ever sting nor harm you
nor create effects to
suffer your body as your reality

anti evolutionaries

humans not living
and demonstrating the change

yet dictating
what must change

are a bane
on humanity

and shall be taken
out of their own way as things unfold
and clear ones step out and drown them out

the cause of a lie

is its justification
and search for its own truth

one human thought
changes the world

is space
having it

come rain or shine

care about what
you thought of yourself

when you
are not thinking

not what you
think at yourself
now you are

the reclamation

the natural order
of evolution

is absolute
spatial chaos

perfectly balanced

and what humans
have been making of space

is exactly what space is
throwing up in opposition
to its self

you have no way back

did space begin
somewhere else

or is it beginning
where it is now

light travels
through space

as space

not
as light

the sky does not rain

the
clouds do

your light

not cry

your
thoughts do

does it not strike you as odd

how humans ask
others to verify what they mean

and go on to blame them
for not being able to
grasp the explanation

says

it is somebody elses fault
i do not understand my self

crazy yet normalized
human behaviour

cut through

looking for your
eye with what is in it

is how you
are blinding yourself

your body dies

because you
are not made of it

setting you off

do words
upset you

you have to question
what you are saying
to yourself with them

not what they
seem to mean

coming from
another source

human doing

how
are you being

not

how are you doing

implies one must
be doing to be

what a self is not

the self
is all you can
not make of you

exposes and unearths
the non self

is your light nature
causing you to have
and live a so called self

you are always
receiving what you wish

through what
you do not want

can you not stop
wanting what you
do not have

test dummies

you can not drive
another persons attitude

without crashing
your car

how to die in a body

being
lived death

is not
dying to it

takes great wisdom and allowing
to not live your human self

and be charged
and lived by space

is

tipping the balance

being able to fit the whole of you
into your own mind with no one else in there
to take the wrap for being you
brings you freedom

owning it all
yet not allowing
it all become you

is the work of
clearing out the closet

a question and an answer

are constructed
by the one mind
thinking it is two

are you an internal
external thinker and mind
you will not understand this

are you a mind
observing your own thought
but not buying into it
you will

be given to

and it wont
feel so taken

give
of your self

and it will
feel like it is being
torn from you

aint it cracked

how human minds think space must
provide proof its alive

how much of you is dead

determines
how much you is alive

double standards

the reason you are
not being all you could be

is because
you are being all you
think you are not being

gum lines

life will bite you
for playing with its teeth

and drown you
for trying not to swim

not that
nature is cruel

just that it backs
up your wanting not to be lived

you can not have life and live without it

is what humans have been doing
in regards to what it makes of itself

not space living it

the depth of co dependancy

a human child
groomed to believe it is not being
and living its own body

leads to an adult
easily controlled and manipulated
by the thought it is anothers

you are not
feeling peoples pain

you are feeling
your own thought about it

is not coming
from their body

the knotted mind

you know
a dark mind is at play

by the way it defends what
it thinks it knows best

shows that it is not mature enough
to own up to knowing anything it might not

holding your charge

you have no need
to know are you alright a light

gives you reason
not to be

no skin in the game

it is best
to let others inclined to try
and win over their self as you

do just that

and carry on not being
them as your self

god speak

shall not
ever turn up
on an empty page

light write
only

losing the plot

it is completely fine
to lose the rag at what you can not see

cradles and soothes your
child throwing a tantrum

not ever
losing it back

the gamet

you might not agree
with some body as your self

and that is
all human

but one must agree
with your self as every body

or its game
over for you

do not know at
the ones out of wack

why

because
it becomes you

code of conduct

you are not being a true
human being

in a reflective
and reactionary mode

know not i

space will not ever show
you what you are not being

is why it hurts so bad
not being it

who you talk to is you

and is that
not clearly understood

then you
are living you dead

the orakhal series
available @ orakhal.com

Printed in Great Britain
by Amazon